Instant Social Media Marketing with HootSuite

Manage and enhance your social media marketing with HootSuite

Kunal Mathur

BIRMINGHAM - MUMBAI

Instant Social Media Marketing with HootSuite

First published: October 2013

Production Reference: 1241013

Published by Packt Publishing Ltd.
Livery Place
35 Livery Street
Birmingham B3 2PB, UK.

ISBN 978-1-84969-666-1

www.packtpub.com

Credits

Author
Kunal Mathur

Reviewers
Catherine Arizan
Jason Schmitt

Acquisition Editors
Saleem Ahmed
Kunal Parikh

Commissioning Editor
Poonam Jain

Technical Editors
Pramod Kumavat
Adrian Raposo

Project Coordinator
Joel Goveya

Copy Editor
Alisha Aranha

Proofreader
Joanna McMahon

Production Coordinator
Nitesh Thakur

Cover Work
Nitesh Thakur

Cover Image
Conidon Miranda

About the Author

Kunal Mathur is a digital marketer specializing in the social media domain. He holds a Post Graduate Diploma in Management and also possesses a Diploma in Advertising and Public Relations. He is a HootSuite Certified Professional and also has expertise in other known tools for social media listening, reputation management, and competitive assessment. He has been active in the field of social media for almost a decade through various social networking sites.

He is currently working in a US-based multinational company, and is handling a social media team and projects in his current role. His interests lie in philately, chess, and learning various marketing software and tools.

I want to thank my parents, sister, and brother-in-law who encouraged and supported me, in spite of all the time it took me away from them.

I would like to thank Packt Publishing for enabling me to write and publish this book, with special thanks to Ameya, Joel, and Poonam for answering my endless questions and helping me throughout this process of book writing.

About the Reviewers

Catherine Arizan is a digital communications strategist with a strong background in social media marketing. She is currently managing the marketing department at Animatron, a Boston-based software startup developing HTML5 animation tools.

Jason Schmitt is an Assistant Professor/Director of Communication Studies at Green Mountain College in Poultney, Vermont. Jason is a seasoned professor bringing with him a wealth of knowledge and experience within the areas of communication, media, social media, journalism, new technology, and regional creativity.

Jason was one of the first educators in the country to partner with HootSuite University, offering students the chance to become Certified HootSuite Professionals. He is a regular contributor, focused towards technology and media for the *Huffington Post*. Jason's first book *Speaking with a Purpose* came out in 2013 for all global markets through Pearson Publishing.

www.PacktPub.com

Support files, eBooks, discount offers and more

You might want to visit www.PacktPub.com for support files and downloads related to your book.

Did you know that Packt offers eBook versions of every book published, with PDF and ePub files available? You can upgrade to the eBook version at www.PacktPub.com and as a print book customer, you are entitled to a discount on the eBook copy. Get in touch with us at service@packtpub.com for more details.

At www.PacktPub.com, you can also read a collection of free technical articles, sign up for a range of free newsletters and receive exclusive discounts and offers on Packt books and eBooks.

http://PacktLib.PacktPub.com

Do you need instant solutions to your IT questions? PacktLib is Packt's online digital book library. Here, you can access, read and search across Packt's entire library of books.

Why Subscribe?

- ▶ Fully searchable across every book published by Packt
- ▶ Copy and paste, print and bookmark content
- ▶ On demand and accessible via web browser

Free Access for Packt account holders

If you have an account with Packt at www.PacktPub.com, you can use this to access PacktLib today and view nine entirely free books. Simply use your login credentials for immediate access.

Table of Contents

Preface   1

Instant Social Media Marketing with HootSuite   5
  Creating your HootSuite account (Simple)   5
  Setting up your HootSuite account (Simple)   7
  Adding and managing profiles (Simple)   10
  Using App Directory (Advanced)   12
  Managing contacts and Twitter lists (Simple)   17
  Using HootSuite for posting – increasing social
  engagement (Simple)   20
  Using RSS feeds and checking user profiles and
  conversations (Intermediate)   26
  Creating teams and assigning tasks (Advanced)   30
  Generating reports using HootSuite Analytics (Intermediate)   35
  Implementing additional options to excel in social media (Advanced) 45

Preface

If you are a marketer who manages and tracks multiple social media profiles, such as LinkedIn, Twitter, and Facebook for your organization, this book is for you. All these social media platforms are generally updated and managed from their respective websites, which takes a lot of time to post on each one of them individually. Creating reports and managing them becomes difficult, as marketers have to collect statistics and data from all social profiles separately, and then evaluate them after proper compilation. All this and more can be easily done and managed from a single social media management tool, HootSuite. This tool helps to post on all social profiles, schedule comments, track links, create reports, and a lot more to excel in social media marketing.

What this book covers

Creating your HootSuite account (Simple), explains about various plans and features that HootSuite offers to marketers. It briefly explains and helps you to choose the best plan as per your requirement.

Setting up your HootSuite account (Simple), teaches you about setting up your account in a step-by-step task, and managing your profiles with HootSuite. This recipe will also teach you about some settings that will help you customize your accounts to your needs and preferences.

Adding and managing profiles (Simple), teaches about connecting your social media assets and managing them from HootSuite. This recipe also explains about connecting multiple accounts of the same or different social media websites.

Using App Directory (Advanced), teaches about integrating apps and connecting to even more social platforms such as YouTube, Instagram, Tumblr, Google+, and so on, or other online tools, such as RSS Reader, Evernote, SurveyMonkey, TrendSpottr, Flickr, and so on.

Managing contacts and Twitter lists (Simple), will teach you the skills of managing Twitter lists and contacts. You will learn to follow, unfollow, and block contacts directly from HootSuite.

Using HootSuite for posting – increasing social engagement (Simple), teaches about posting on multiple social assets at the same time. You will also learn about using advance options, such as scheduling, privacy, location, link preview, and drafts.

Using RSS feeds and checking user profiles and conversations (Intermediate), teaches about connecting your company's blog with social media accounts to directly share articles at specific timings. Also learn about checking user profiles and details directly from HootSuite.

Creating teams and assigning tasks (Advanced), teaches how to create teams to manage and collaborate with other social marketers at your organization, and assigning tasks between your team members and tracking the actions taken on each task.

Generating reports using HootSuite Analytics (Intermediate), will teach you how to create reports and charts using the data shared and posted from HootSuite. Get detailed analysis and reports to plan your future social media campaigns.

Implementing additional options to excel in social media (Advanced), contains some general tips and tricks of the industry that will help you become a better social media marketer.

What you need for this book

You will need active accounts and basic knowledge about various social media platforms, such as LinkedIn, Twitter, Facebook, and Google+.

Who this book is for

This book is for all those marketing professionals who have an interest in social media marketing and are working in this domain. This is for a marketer who wants to learn about HootSuite—a social media management tool that helps in managing, tracking, and reporting social activities of their profile and brands.

Conventions

In this book, you will find a number of styles of text that distinguish between different kinds of information. Here are some examples of these styles and an explanation of their meaning.

Code words in text are shown as follows: "you can insert `Read our new article:`, which automatically appears before each blog post".

New terms and **important words** are shown in bold. Words that you see on the screen, in menus or dialog boxes for example, appear in the text like this: "Additional social profiles can be connected by clicking on the **Add Social Network** button".

[Warnings or important notes appear in a box like this.]

[Tips and tricks appear like this.]

Reader feedback

Feedback from our readers is always welcome. Let us know what you think about this book—what you liked or may have disliked. Reader feedback is important for us to develop titles that you really get the most out of.

To send us general feedback, simply send an e-mail to feedback@packtpub.com, and mention the book title via the subject of your message.

If there is a topic that you have expertise in and you are interested in either writing or contributing to a book, see our author guide on www.packtpub.com/authors.

Customer support

Now that you are the proud owner of a Packt book, we have a number of things to help you to get the most from your purchase.

Errata

Although we have taken every care to ensure the accuracy of our content, mistakes do happen. If you find a mistake in one of our books—maybe a mistake in the text or the code—we would be grateful if you would report this to us. By doing so, you can save other readers from frustration and help us improve subsequent versions of this book. If you find any errata, please report them by visiting http://www.packtpub.com/submit-errata, selecting your book, clicking on the **errata submission form** link, and entering the details of your errata. Once your errata are verified, your submission will be accepted and the errata will be uploaded on our website, or added to any list of existing errata, under the Errata section of that title. Any existing errata can be viewed by selecting your title from http://www.packtpub.com/support.

Piracy

Piracy of copyright material on the Internet is an ongoing problem across all media. At Packt, we take the protection of our copyright and licenses very seriously. If you come across any illegal copies of our works, in any form, on the Internet, please provide us with the location address or website name immediately so that we can pursue a remedy.

Please contact us at `copyright@packtpub.com` with a link to the suspected pirated material.

We appreciate your help in protecting our authors, and our ability to bring you valuable content.

Questions

You can contact us at `questions@packtpub.com` if you are having a problem with any aspect of the book, and we will do our best to address it.

Instant Social Media Marketing with HootSuite

Welcome to *Instant Social Media Marketing with HootSuite*. This book is an explanatory guide to HootSuite and its features. This book will help marketers to manage their multiple social media profiles and create reports to track client engagement.

Creating your HootSuite account (Simple)

HootSuite is a social media management tool that helps you to manage multiple social networks, and offers direct support for Twitter, Facebook, LinkedIn, Google+, Foursquare, and WordPress from a single dashboard. Its **Apps** feature allows you to integrate with Gmail, YouTube, Flickr, Tumblr, Instagram, Evernote, SlideShare, Vimeo, Storify, StumbleUpon, reddit, among others. We will learn several possible options to create a HootSuite account.

Getting ready

A marketer needs to have an account on any of the previously-stated social media platforms.

How to do it...

1. Go to `http://www.hootsuite.com/` and sign up from your Facebook account or by entering your e-mail address, full name, and desired password.

2. You will find three plans: Free, Pro, and Enterprise. For the purpose of this example, we will select Pro.

3. Select from an **Annual** or **Monthly** payment option and provide payment details to create the account.

How it works...

Go to `http://www.hootsuite.com/` and you will see the **Sign Up** section to the right that allows you to instantly create a HootSuite account using your Twitter or Facebook login. Alternatively, you can also use your full name and an e-mail address to create an account.

It is advisable to sign up on HootSuite using the latter option as it provides an the advantage of creating a completely new password for managing your account. This works as an additional security to all linked social profiles that you are planning to link with this tool. You can refer to the following screenshot for reference:

HootSuite provides plans and features that suit individuals, SMEs, and large-scale organizations, depending upon their social activities. The available plans can be seen at `http://signup.hootsuite.com/plans-cc/`. HootSuite's **FREE** plan allows you to connect up to five social profiles and generate basic analytics reports, whereas a **PRO** account allows you to connect to 50 social profiles, Google Analytics and Facebook Insight integration, detailed reports, and an additional user. You also get a 30-day free trial with your **PRO** plan.

You can select between **Monthly** or **Annual** payment options and can get a 10 percent discount while opting for the latter method. You can make the payment through your credit card or PayPal account.

Setting up your HootSuite account (Simple)

We will learn about setting up a HootSuite account before we actually start using it.

How to do it...

1. Select **Settings** from the left ribbon to open the **Settings** window.
2. Upload your **Profile Image**, enter your **Full Name**, **Initials**, **Time Zone**, and other details under the **Account** section.
3. Add additional authentication methods.
4. Update notification settings in the **Notifications** section.

How it works...

Select **Settings** from the left selection ribbon to open the pop-up window. You can change HootSuite account settings to improve your experience of using this tool. You can upload your image, enter your full name and initials, e-mail ID (if you created the account using Facebook), bio/description, and other details.

Check the **Auto initial when composing messages** checkbox to enable HootSuite to pre-populate tweets with your initials in the **Compose Message...** section. This feature is helpful when you are working in groups, and multiple users are replying on Twitter from their individual HootSuite accounts.

You can update the **Time Zone** that your HootSuite dashboard is following by selecting the correct time zone you are in. You can also update your Twitter, Facebook, LinkedIn, and Google+ account links in the description. Entering profile links will not connect your accounts with HootSuite but are just updated for reference.

You can change the password of your HootSuite account from the same tab. Please note that this option can be used if you have used your e-mail to create the account.

Additionally, you can also add more **Authentication Methods** in the **Authentication** tab and simplify the login process by using third-party accounts such as Google, Yahoo, and OpenID.

You can set general preferences and notifications for your HootSuite account by clicking on **Preferences**, as shown in the following screenshot:

In the **Preferences** section, you will be able to select your preferred language for your HootSuite account.

 Please note that this language selection is limited to your HootSuite login and does not extend to any of your social profiles.

When you like a tweet, you simply click on the retweet button to share it on your timeline. This does not allow you to add, comment, or edit the tweet before sharing it with your followers. However, if you unselect **Use Twitter Web retweets**, then the text from the tweet will appear in the **Compose Message...** field starting with **RT @username** and you can edit it with your views or comments before sharing.

Twitter allows companies to promote the tweets that are visible on the top of your Twitter stream; however, you can hide promotional tweets in HootSuite by unselecting the respective option from the **Preferences** tab. This feature is only available to Pro users.

The **Preferences** tab also allows you to select a theme (from the **Themes** tab) for a HootSuite account between **Blue Steel**, **Classic**, and **Magnum**.

You can also modify your e-mail and HootSuite dashboard notification settings by going to the **Notifications** tab. You should opt to receive a weekly account activity report that is directly delivered to you in your registered mailbox. You can also select to receive the latest news and announcements from HootSuite on your registered e-mail and stay updated with the recent changes. Checking the **Play a sound and flash the title bar when new messages appear in my streams** checkbox proves helpful while working on multiple tabs of your browser.

You can also set **Alerts and Notifications** to send an e-mail or play a sound whenever someone likes or comments on your posts. In addition, you can subscribe to a daily e-mail digest with the recent conversations over your posts.

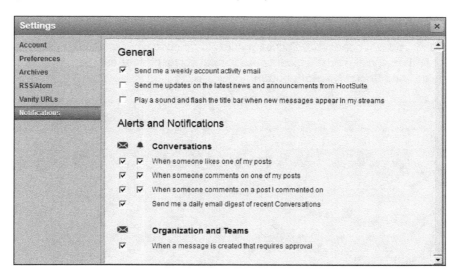

Adding and managing profiles (Simple)

In this recipe, you will learn how to add social media profiles and manage them in streams and tabs.

How to do it...

1. Click on **Add Social Network**.
2. Select from the available options of social media platforms.
3. Connect using a simple authorization method.
4. Add multiple social media profiles.
5. Create different streams for different types of conversations by clicking on **Add Stream**.
6. Create different tabs to add more social media profiles.

How it works...

You can directly connect Twitter, Facebook, Google+, LinkedIn, Foursquare, WordPress, and MySpace. You can log in and integrate these social networks from the same screen by clicking on **Add Social Network**.

As a Free user you can connect five social profiles at no cost, whereas all Pro users can connect unlimited social media accounts. Additional social profiles can be connected by clicking on the **Add Social Network** button.

After connecting your profiles, you can check them at the top-left corner of the dashboard.

There are various ways to manage the look of your dashboard. HootSuite gives you the flexibility to manage your social profiles in tabs and streams. Tabs are separators for organizing your social profiles. They are used to create and manage streams, which are columns to classify your feeds, posts, direct messages, and so on. See the preceding screenshot for a better understanding.

As a HootSuite user you can add up to 20 tabs with 10 streams each.

It is recommended that you create separate tabs for different social profiles such as Twitter, Facebook, and LinkedIn. This will enable you to manage them separately. An example of this is shown in the following screenshot:

All connected social networks will show your profile picture at the top-right corner of the dashboard. These icons are also used to post comments on a specific social profile. You may also note that I have created different tabs in the preceding screenshot that enable me to browse specific content in their respective streams.

For Twitter profiles, you can create separate streams for **Home Feed** (Twitter timeline), direct messages received, direct messages sent, tweets sent by you, tweets mentioning your Twitter handle, your tweets that have been retweeted by other users, tweets that you've marked as favorites, and any tweet scheduled by you to be posted at any future time using HootSuite.

You can create various streams to view your Facebook profile for wall posts, as visible on `https://www.facebook.com` or the most recent status updates, photos, and video filters. You can also manage separate streams for events and scheduled messages.

Businesses can also manage Facebook pages from HootSuite and create streams for wall posts, private messages sent by customers and prospects, and their events. Once you have connected your Facebook page with HootSuite, if you like to schedule messages and comments to go out at a specified time, you can create a separate stream for the same.

If you own or manage a company page on LinkedIn, there are two streams that can be created: **Company** updates and **Scheduled** updates.

Similarly, if you own or manage LinkedIn Groups, you can create **All** discussions, **Most Popular** discussions, and **Scheduled** updates.

There's more...

By default, all streams refresh every five minutes; however, you can change and choose between various predefined time intervals of 2, 5, 10, 15, or 30 minutes. Alternatively, you have a manual refresh icon that lets you update your stream whenever you want.

Using App Directory (Advanced)

This recipe will teach you how to integrate various social content applications directly from HootSuite.

How to do it...

1. Move the cursor on the left ribbon.
2. Select **App Directory** to open a new window.
3. Select the required app/plugin and integrate available social content apps within HootSuite's web-based dashboard.

How it works...

Select the **App Directory** option from HootSuite's left ribbon and it will open a dialogue box with a list of apps that can be integrated with HootSuite. Currently, HootSuite allows you to connect with more than 55 social media networks. Most of the apps are free to connect, however, few premium apps have also been provided. They generally cost around $1.99 to $4.99 per month.

Some of the premium apps that can be integrated by all types of users are Statigram, YouTube, Salesforce, and TrendSpottr. HubSpot and SocialFlow are the two premium apps that are only available to Pro and Enterprise HootSuite users.

As discussed in the beginning of the book, a few commonly used social networking websites can be integrated with HootSuite using app integration, such as Instagram, Tumblr, YouTube, SlideShare, Reddit, Vimeo, Flickr, Evernote, Storify, and StumbleUpon.

You can simply click on **Install App** to integrate them with the HootSuite account. Once integrated, you can create a stream within any of the existing tabs or create new tabs for any specific app.

Some of the apps will be standalone, whereas a few will require your login details, such as YouTube and Instagram.

There's more...

Let's discuss the few less-known, but important, apps that can be used by marketers using HootSuite.

Evernote

Evernote allows users to capture, organize, and find information from multiple platforms. Evernote is a widely used application because it works on almost all computers, mobile devices, and tablets. The Evernote app allows its users to search content from social networks using keywords. You can view, edit, and share notes with those on your social networks using HootSuite integration.

RSS Reader

You can add RSS feeds in the RSS Reader app and start receiving articles or information directly on your HootSuite dashboard. You can rename this stream as well so that you can manage multiple streams, receiving information from different sources.

If you already have an OPML file, you can import multiple feeds and get a stream of articles. As this app is integrated within HootSuite, it allows you to share the articles on your social networks as well.

TrendSpottr

TrendSpottr is one of the best apps that we have seen recently. It lets you find trending topics from across social networks. The TrendSpottr app allows you to search for trending content using a keyword/phrase, topic, or type such as trending content, trending hashtags, or trending sources.

You can also pick from predefined topics—news, technology, social media, infographic, economy, sports, pop culture, politics, science, and celebrity—or from a list of popular searches. You can share the trending content with your social networks right from this app integrated with HootSuite.

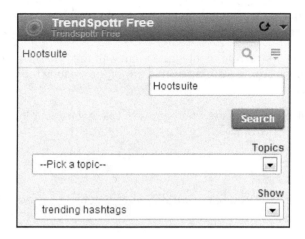

YouTube

As a digital marketer, you always want to post videos about your products, features, client testimonials, and other visuals to stay connected with your clients. You can connect multiple YouTube accounts at a monthly price of $1.99. Create a separate tab to share and schedule videos from your YouTube account. You can add a title, description, video tags, and privacy settings, and assign a category to your video before uploading.

You can also create streams to search and monitor any specific channel, uploader information, or subscriptions. This proves very helpful to share any YouTube video on your other social profiles connected with HootSuite.

YouTube Analytics

Once you integrate your YouTube account and channel with HootSuite, you can view all analytics from the dashboard itself by integrating the free analytics app (paid app with more insights also available).

You can view details about your videos and channels with video-based insights such as engagement levels, sources and countries of traffic, playbacks, demographics and geographic information. You can use all the insights available on the YouTube website.

Flickr

Just like videos being shared on YouTube, some organizations share pictures of their employees, products, and so on over Flickr. HootSuite offers the ability to integrate using the Flickr app that allows you to view images, upload new pictures, search for pictures, and share them on other connected social media profiles such as Twitter and Facebook.

SurveyMonkey

As a marketer, you always want to interact with your followers and have an ongoing need to take their feedback. SurveyMonkey is a one-stop solution for feedback from not only your Twitter followers, but also your prospects and customers through e-mails and other online channels. This app allows you to track the created surveys and share them with your social networks.

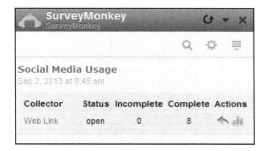

Responses in SurveyMonkey's stream on HootSuite's dashboard are updated on a real-time basis. Once you start receiving responses, you can view responses in a question-summary form that pop up after clicking on the bar graph icon under the **Actions** label, as seen in the preceding screenshot.

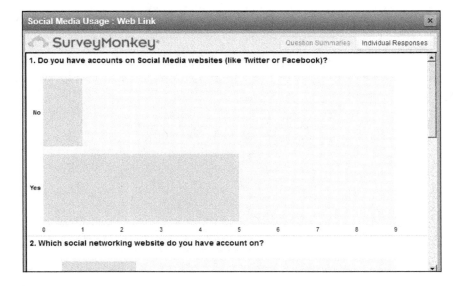

You can also see detailed replies by all the respondents after switching to the **Individual Responses** tab as shown in the following screenshot:

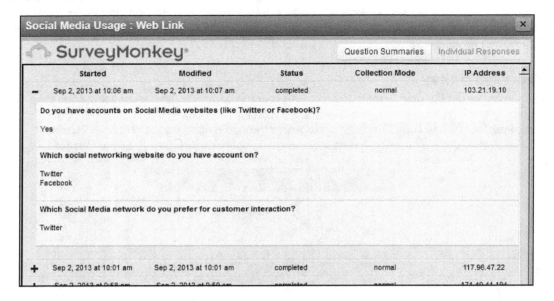

SlideShare

Marketing, sales, training, and support teams of organizations create PDFs, presentations, and documents to keep their clients or employees abreast with recent happenings. This SlideShare app that gets integrated with HootSuite provides easy access to view complete presentations and search documents on the basis of keywords. It also allows the sharing of such documents over other social media platforms that are connected to HootSuite.

List of apps

For the updated list of app directories that can be integrated with HootSuite's web-based social profile management tool, you can visit `http://hootsuite.com/app-directory`.

Managing contacts and Twitter lists (Simple)

It is important to know your followers or connections on social profiles. In this recipe, we will learn to manage Twitter contacts as Twitter lists and follow/unfollow them.

How to do it...

1. Go to **Contacts** on the left dashboard ribbon.

2. Select your connected Twitter account to view all followers and their details.

3. Select **Lists** from the dropdown and check all profiles of a Twitter list.

4. Use Contact Management options to follow and unfollow profiles directly from HootSuite.

How it works...

HootSuite has a contact management feature that lets you follow, unfollow, or list your Twitter followers and those who you follow. This can be accessed from the left navigation pane by selecting **Contacts** as shown in the following screenshot:

You will be able to see the listing of people you follow and those following you, with their respective following and followers count. You can also see their Klout score, which is an indicator of a person's social presence measured on a scale of 0 to 100. A higher Klout score is considered as good and that a Twitter user is active and has followers who share and reply to the tweets. See the following screenshot for a better understanding:

You can also follow/unfollow Twitter handles directly from HootSuite by clicking on the symbol placed before the **Following** stats.

When you start following hundreds of Twitter profiles, it becomes difficult to get the relevant tweets from specific people. In such scenarios, Twitter lists allow users to create a group of Twitter accounts that they want to see regularly and read their tweets in one place.

It has to be noted that lists can only be used for reading tweets. You cannot send tweets to members of a list, considering that only list members will be able to see it. The name of the list cannot start with a number and has to be done alphabetically. By default, lists are public and are visible to everyone. Lists can also be made private by changing their individual settings.

Lists are useful because you do not have to follow a Twitter user before adding them to the lists. However, you cannot add those users to your lists who have blocked you on Twitter. Similarly, if someone has added you to their list, you can block the list's creator to remove yourself.

You can create a list of the clients, partners, friends, industry experts, or any group of Twitter accounts that are relevant to you. Also, you can subscribe to lists created by other users if the Twitter accounts in those lists make sense to you.

In a couple of the following screenshots, you will note that we have created four lists out of which two are private (with a padlock sign). Lists named as **Twitter Accounts** and **Social Media and News** are public and can be read or subscribed to by any Twitter user.

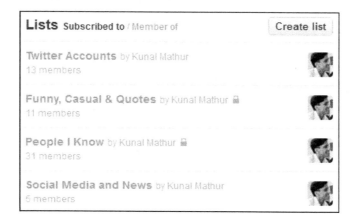

We may miss out on news or information about social media as we generally follow many Twitter accounts. So to avoid such situations and to stay updated with the recent happenings in the world of social media, we can create a list of Twitter accounts (industry experts and magazines) that provide us with a daily dose of information. As the list is public, there are other people as well who may subscribe to these lists.

You can manage Twitter lists from HootSuite itself by adding or removing their members. This can be done by clicking and dragging them to the desired lists.

In addition to follow/unfollow and adding/removing members from lists, you can also block Twitter users and report them as spam from HootSuite itself. This can be done by using the small arrow icon under each user thumbnail.

Using HootSuite for posting – increasing social engagement (Simple)

We will learn various ways to post on social media platforms, using additional features and scheduling of tweets.

How to do it...

1. Tweet/post on various social media profiles.
2. Use location, privacy options, and link preview for Facebook.

How it works...

This recipe will equip you for using social network selection and **Compose message...** options.

At the top of your HootSuite dashboard, you can see the ribbon as shown in the preceding screenshot that is used for composing a message, attaching files, selecting privacy settings, and many other options, which are very useful for marketers while posting on social networks. If you click anywhere on the blank area of this ribbon, it drops down and displays options, which we'll discuss now.

Let's learn about each numbered icon from the preceding screenshot:

1. Using the **Add a link...** field, you can share any link from the web and post it through your social profiles. HootSuite allows you to shrink the URL using its own URL shorteners: **ow.ly**, **owl.li**, **ht.ly**, and **htl.li** (the latter two commonly pronounced as Hoot-ly). You can choose one of these by clicking on the small wheel icon just to the left of the **Shrink** button, as shown in the following screenshot:

Use **ht.ly** when you want to use HootSuite's Social Bar at the top of your browser page, and use **ow.ly** when you want your links to appear without their Social Bar.

Anything posted via HootSuite using **ht.ly** will have a Social Bar, as shown in the previous screenshot, that lets you forward posts, articles, and so on via Twitter, Facebook, Digg, and several other options.

2. Using the **Attach image or file** icon, you can share any video, audio, or document saved on your system from your social profiles. When you click on this icon, it further drops down, allowing you to either drop files directly from your desktop or by using the **Select files to upload** button to browse the desired file from your computer.

Once the file gets uploaded, it automatically creates a shortened URL of the image or file and you can add a caption or title of the file before actually posting it on your social profiles. HootSuite also allows you to hide a URL while posting it on Facebook or Google+ profiles.

3. After composing your message and selecting the desired social media profile, HootSuite allows you to schedule, autoschedule, or post the message right away on your social profiles. This is one of the most important and helpful tools for any marketer, as they can time their message to go out at a specified time and don't have to be present in front of their system at all times.

By clicking on the **Scheduling** icon, you can open a drop-down window wherein you can select the desired date and time for your message to be posted and then click on the **Schedule** button. In case you are not sure about the time zone that your HootSuite dashboard is following, then go to **Settings | Accounts | Time Zone** to identify and/or edit it.

All scheduled messages can be seen on a single page by going to **Publisher | Scheduled** as shown in the following screenshot. You can filter your scheduled messages by list, day, week, and month or by social media profile. Every message can be edited or deleted from this screen in addition to changing its time of publishing or social profiles. At the bottom-left corner of the screen, you can see the current time and time zone being followed by HootSuite.

You can also export your scheduled messages in CSV or Google CSV format.

If you are unaware of the optimal time of posting a message on your social profiles, you can also autoschedule your posts. After writing a message, select a desired social profile and click on the **Scheduling** icon; you can toggle the **AutoSchedule** switch to **On** and then click on the **AutoSchedule** button. The autoscheduling feature determines the best time to share messages from your social profiles on the basis of RT, replies, favorites, and the clicks your tweets receive from your followers at certain hours. This feature programs itself to send your tweets at the best time. Though it is not possible to accurately identify the best time to tweet, the autoschedule feature is still a useful tool.

You can view all such messages from the same location as scheduled messages; however, autoscheduled messages have a clock icon before its time of posting.

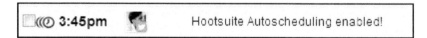

These messages are similar to scheduled messages and can be edited, rescheduled, or deleted at any time. After rescheduling, the clock icon disappears as an indicator that it has been manually scheduled.

4. Adding a location to your messages allows your followers and friends to see where you are while messaging. This feature requires permission to access your location.

This feature is useful for businesses who want to drive customers to their shops by posting locations with their messages.

5.   HootSuite allows you to use privacy options for Facebook, Google+, and LinkedIn. This option can be activated by clicking on the padlock icon, which further opens a drop-down panel. This panel will show you the privacy options as per the social media profiles selected by you.

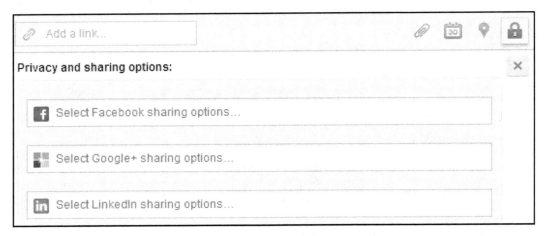

While posting on Facebook, you can either post with **Public** settings, that is, visible to all users, or make your post visible to a specific list created on Facebook. You can share updates with **Connections only** or **Anyone** when you are updating your LinkedIn status message. Similarly, HootSuite's privacy option for Google+ allows you to share your posts with public, specific circles, all of your circles, or extended circles. This helps you to viral your messages to the target group.

6.   If you have written a message but are not ready to send it right away, you can click on the floppy disk icon to save it as a draft. If you have selected a social profile on which you want to post this message, it will also get saved in drafts, allowing for faster sharing at a later point in time. You can save a message only if there is one social profile selected.

The arrowhead next to the floppy disk icon shows all your saved messages. You can click on any saved draft message and it will come up in the **Compose message...** box, wherein you can edit the content, select more social profiles, and post it by clicking the **Send Now** button. You can also delete any saved draft message by clicking the trash bin icon.

7. The **Pin** feature allows you to set default social profiles that will always populate in the profile selector bar by clicking the **Pin** icon. It will change in shape when pinned and will start showing in the profile selection bar. You can also pin multiple social profiles that are linked with HootSuite. In case you do not want to share any message with a pinned profile, click on the profile selection bar before clicking on the **Send Now** button.

    To unpin a social profile, you have to click on its icon to remove it from the profile selection bar. Then, click on the **Pin** icon to unpin it. All unpinned social profiles have to be manually selected before posting comments on them.

8. If you are managing multiple social profiles, you can mark your favorite ones from the profile selection dropdown. This feature helps you to access the most commonly used profiles and saves you time in searching from the list. You can click on the star icon available to the left of the **Pin** icon. The blank star will convert to a yellow-colored star, which is an indication of the **Favorite** profile.

You can see only **Favorites** by clicking on the dropdown present at the bottom-right corner of the profile selection. Select **Favorites** in it. You can then click on the desired social profile to post comments on it.

Using RSS feeds and checking user profiles and conversations (Intermediate)

This topic will teach marketers to link RSS feeds with their social profiles, understanding fans and followers, and getting involved in conversations.

How to do it...

1. Set automatic tweeting using RSS/Atom Feeds.

2. Check user profiles and other details directly from HootSuite by clicking on their profiles.

3. Reply to and read complete conversations from HootSuite by using **View conversations**.

How it works...

If you have multiple blogs and want to publish those articles directly on your social profiles as well, go to **Settings** and then click on **RSS/Atom**. This allows you to share your blog posts automatically across your networks.

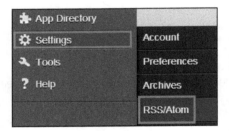

It will open another dialog box wherein you have to input the RSS feed URL; the network on which you want to share posts; how frequently you want HootSuite to check for new posts (minimum is one hour); and if new posts are found, how many of them should be shared from your social profile (maximum is five posts at a time).

The most useful feature of this function is that you can add 20 characters of text before each blog post. For example, you can insert `Read our new article:`, which automatically appears before each blog post shared on the social profiles; or if you are sharing content from other sources, you can add `Blog post via @mashable:` so that they know that you are sharing their posts.

The free version allows you to share one blog using RSS; however, the paid version at $8.99 a month allows you unlimited blogs. Once you are connected to multiple blogs from your social accounts, you can view all of them from the RSS page.

Let us look at some of the important aspects of **RSS/Atom Feeds** (numbered in red in the preceding screenshot):

1. Name and link to the RSS URL can be seen in the **Details** section.

2. This image shows the profile on which the posts will be shared and can be seen in the **Target** section.

3. You can edit or delete any RSS feed whenever required. In case an organization changes its blog address or RSS location, you can change the settings. You can also edit the frequency of checking and sharing the RSS feeds from this location.

4. You can use these switches to enable or disable RSS feeds without actually deleting them.

Checking a user's profile and other details

HootSuite enables users to check details of other Twitter users right from the dashboard. When a user clicks on any Twitter handle (username) from the HootSuite dashboard, it opens a pop-up box that shows a user's followers, following, updates (tweets), and Klout scores. It also provides information that has been updated on Twitter. Users can click on other tabs of the pop-up box to view a user's **Timeline Mentions** and **Favorites**.

You can also read tweets that have been favorited by the user by clicking on the **Favorites** tab. Marketers can also follow, unfollow, reply, or add a user to a specific list from the options provided at the bottom of the pop-up box. If the other Twitter user is following you, a **DM** (Direct Message) can also be sent. A direct message works as an e-mail within Twitter and is only visible to the sender and receiver of the messages. It is mandatory for the receiver to follow a sender's Twitter profile for interaction through direct messages.

Instant replies to queries is very important for all businesses. When a marketer takes the cursor to the top-right corner of any tweet within HootSuite, it starts showing a few icons. These icons are **Reply**, **Retweet**, **Direct Message**, **Reply All**, **Favorite**, **Send to Email**, and **Send to Conversation...**.

When you click on the **Reply** icon, the Twitter handle from the tweet automatically gets pasted in **Compose message...**, allowing you to write a reply and send.

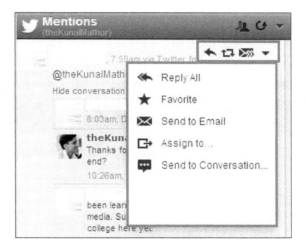

You can also read the conversation that happened between you and your clients or prospects without leaving the HootSuite dashboard. This functionality helps marketers to provide prompt replies to clients' problems or queries and reduce any time lag in responses. When you click on **Show Conversation**, it provides a drop-down menu and marketers will be able to see the complete conversation.

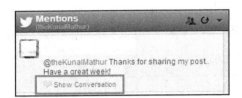

Creating teams and assigning tasks (Advanced)

This recipe will teach us how to create teams on HootSuite for managing outgoing messages and assigning tasks to them.

How to do it...

1. Go to the user profile icon at the top-left corner.
2. Create an organization and provide it with a name.
3. Go to **Manage** and create a team by selecting **Add Team.**
4. Add members to the team.
5. Use the **Assign to...** option to directly assign tasks from the dashboard to the team members.

How it works...

If the number of employees handling social media profiles of an organization increases, HootSuite helps in boosting team collaboration. You can create organizations, teams, and social networks or a selection of the three within HootSuite. The teams will have team members with different authority levels. It is important to understand a few terminologies and member roles before going forward.

- ▶ **Default**: This member can only view details about the team they are a part of and social networks they have access to within that organization.

- ▶ **Admin:** This member can invite and manage team members, all teams in the organization and social networks, in addition to all permissions of a default user.

- ▶ **Super admin:** This member has all admin permissions and can also manage other organization decisions such as vanity URLs, archives, enrolment in HootSuite University, and so on.

- ▶ **Social Network**: This member can belong to only one organization and when a team member is added to an organization, they automatically receive default permissions.

- ▶ **Team**: This is a group of users who work together on various social networks within an organization. A team can only be created by a marketer if he/she is a super admin, admin, or team admin. Each team member can be connected to multiple teams and social networks.

- ▶ **Organization**: This, in HootSuite, is the highest entity that has teams, team members, and social networks. Note that each HootSuite user can only create and become the super admin of their own organizations.

As per the structure of HootSuite organizations, if a team member is removed from one role in the organization, the member is not removed from the entire organization. If a team member belongs to a team and a social network and is only removed from the team, he can still access the network, depending on their permission level for the latter. Also, you only add premium members to the teams.

To create a new organization, click on the user profile icon from the top-left corner and then click on the **Start Collaborating with others** button.

This will open a pop-up box where you can provide a name to your organization and upload an image. Click on the **Create Organization** button and you can check your organization name, member role and the number of premium seats used by the user.

To overview the organizational setup, click on the user profile icon at the top-left corner of the dashboard and then click on **Manage**. While on this page, note the highlighted star; it depicts the paying member of the organization. An example of this setup can be seen in the following screenshot:

You will have to create a team by clicking on **Add Team** on the next page and then filling the pop-up box with the team name. You can also upload a team photo, however, it is not mandatory. Click to select one or more members by clicking on **Invite Members**, but note that only members who have been invited to your organization will populate in the list. After inviting members, click on **Add Social Network** to add a social network to this team; however, only those social networks that have been added to your organization will populate in the list.

Clicking on **Create Team** will create a team that can be viewed by clicking on the **Manage** button. The first row will have the team members for that specified team and the bottom row will have the social network.

You can click on the gear icon to view team details, edit settings, or manage permissions of the team members. Once the team has been created and team members are assigned to social networks, marketers can now allocate posts for replies or follow-ups.

Click on the house icon from the left ribbon to go back to the streams.

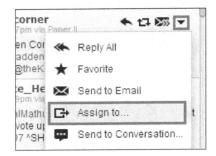

Now, when you find a message that needs to be assigned, click on the arrowhead and select **Assign to....** This will open a pop-up box wherein you can select a team and then select the team member. You can also write an optional comment for the member who will reply as the lead.

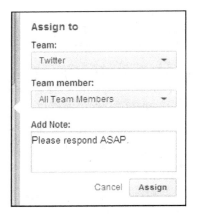

These notes can be seen by everyone in that team. Once the **Assign** button has been clicked, the tweet is highlighted and it starts showing the name of the contact to whom the lead has been assigned. It will also show the comment and time at which the lead was assigned to the team member.

Generating reports using HootSuite Analytics (Intermediate)

After starting engagement on social media via HootSuite, we must track our efforts using various free and paid reports. These reports are really useful to measure results such as audience engagement from our social media activities, mainly undertaken from the HootSuite dashboard. It is very important to gauge how well your content was received by your fans, followers, and other users.

Getting ready

A marketer should have used HootSuite for posting on social media profiles to have adequate data for reports.

How to do it...

HootSuite Analytics can be accessed by clicking on the left-side bar and then selecting the graphics icon as shown in the following screenshot. There are saved templates that can be used for preformatted reports.

HootSuite reports and analytics work on a points-based system. These points can be purchased separately in the final step of completing your analytics reports. A Pro user gets 50 points for generating reports every month. If you are a Free account user, you will be required to upgrade your HootSuite account. Once you have finished adding modules to your report you can see the points counter at the top of your dashboard. If you exceed the available points, as an indicator, the number of points changes to red.

You can generate more than ten types of reports using HootSuite's **Templates**. This gives you an instant overview of what's happening with your social efforts across your Twitter account and Facebook pages.

URL Click Stats - ow.ly provides you with statistics for any URL that has been shortened using HootSuite's in-house URL shortener and shared from its dashboard. This gives you the expanded web location of the link, in addition to the date of creation and total clicks registered on that specific link. You can also see a chart that shows the dates when that link recorded the clicks. In case you do not remember the link, you can search for stats about any `ow.ly` URL shared from your Twitter account by selecting the connected Twitter profile from the dropdown. It will give you details of your complete messages. You can click on the `ow.ly` links to check the engagement from that shortened URL.

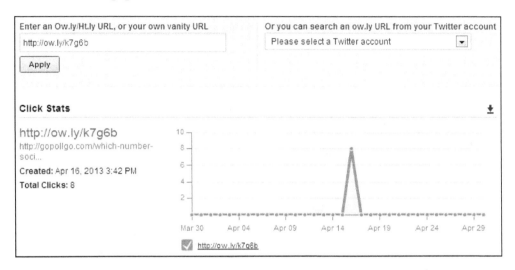

If you want more details and do not want to limit your report to an individual, click on **Ow.ly Click Summary**. It gives you details about the number of links clicked, region of user who clicked the link, top referrer website from where the clicks were registered, and a list of articles that registered the highest clicks. All this information helps you to understand your audience and plan your future messages accordingly.

The following screenshot of **Ow.ly Click Summary** shows how well these statistics are presented by HootSuite Analytics. They are easy to interpret and at the same time provide you with adequate information.

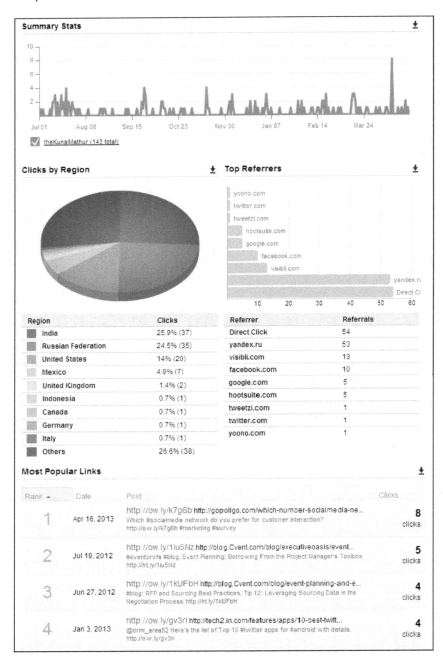

The Facebook Insight report shows similar statistics that are available to a page administrator directly after logging into Facebook. This allows you to identify total likes, new likes, people talking about this, reach, user demographics and location, among others. This is a free report and gives you an instant analysis of your brands' performance on Facebook.

After connecting Google Analytics to HootSuite you can generate reports of your website activity. A Google Analytics report provides you with useful web tracking information. However, you must connect your Google Analytics account to HootSuite before generating the Google Analytics report. This is also a paid report that requires 50 HootSuite points.

In addition to preformatted reports, you can also customize your reports with modules that you would like to see in the reports.

This also enables you to combine Twitter and Facebook stats in the same report. To use this feature, click on **Build Custom Report** under **Customize** and then select **Custom Report**. Start from scratch! And design your custom report.

This will open a new page where you can create a custom report. This page is divided into six major areas, as shown in the following screenshot:

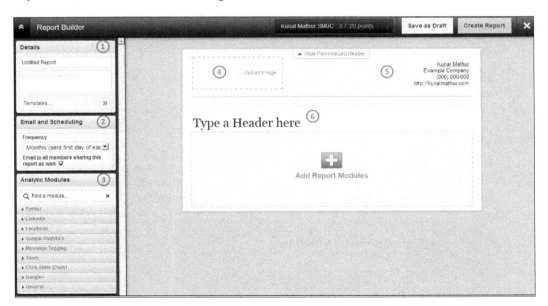

1. The **Details** field is used to label your report so that you can organize different types of reports by their content. The value entered here will not be the title of your report and this information will remain in HootSuite only.

2. You can use the **Email and Scheduling** section to schedule the delivery of reports directly to your mailbox. The frequency can be set to daily, weekly, monthly, twice a month, or no e-mail at all.

3. The **Analytic Modules** section has all the formats that you can use in your report. There are more than 60 modules for Twitter, LinkedIn, Facebook, Google+, and Google Analytics. You can add these modules to the report by simply clicking the faded **+** sign. Please note that some of these modules require points, whereas a few others are limited to Enterprise users.

4. You can upload your company's logo (recommended) or an image that represents the content of this report.

5. Marketers can edit the top-right section to update their name, contact information, company name, address, website, and other such details.

6. The section represented as number **6** in the preceding screenshot contains the header that becomes the title of your report. Generally, marketers mention their organization's name in this section.

Click on **Create Report** once you have added all the required modules and have updated the six sections explained. You'll be sent back to the HootSuite Analytics page, where you can view or edit all reports created by you.

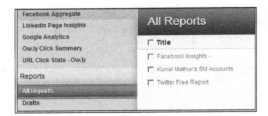

Modules that are available for free to all type a of users are:

► **Profile Summary**: This section of the report shows your number of followers, number of users that you are following, number of lists that you are part of, and your Twitter bio. It is a representation of your Twitter profile.

- **Mentions by Influencers**: It is very important for all marketers to know who is interacting with them on Twitter, retweeting their updates, and mentioning them in the tweets. Marketers should acknowledge them and thank them to make them feel special.

- **Summary Stats**: This section shows the number of clicks on a timeline that helps marketers to identify the best day to send a specific type of message to get maximum clicks.

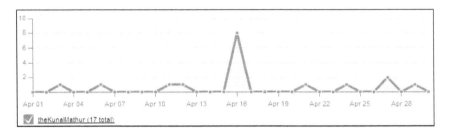

- **Clicks by Region**: The following pie chart tells you about the location of the users who are clicking on the links shared by you. This can also prove helpful in developing campaigns for a specific location from where you are getting maximum clicks.

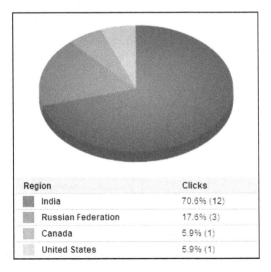

Region	Clicks
India	70.6% (12)
Russian Federation	17.6% (3)
Canada	5.9% (1)
United States	5.9% (1)

► **Top Referrer**: This section shows you which sites sent the most traffic to your links. This can be useful if you use HootSuite to send messages to multiple social networks (Twitter, Facebook, LinkedIn, among others) and to see where your messages are the most effective.

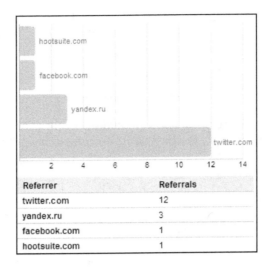

Referrer	Referrals
twitter.com	12
yandex.ru	3
facebook.com	1
hootsuite.com	1

► **Most Popular Links / All Links**: It is very important for marketers to know which specific tweets got the most clicks from the audience. With the help of this information, you can get an idea on topics and subjects that really resonate with your audience. You can also try changing certain word patterns if they are more effective than others.

Rank ▲	Date	Post	Clicks
1	Apr 16, 2013	http://ow.ly/k7g6b http://gopollgo.com/which-number-socialmedia-ne... Which #socialmedia network do you prefer for customer interaction? http://ow.ly/k7g6b #marketing #survey	**8** clicks
2	Apr 9, 2013	http://ow.ly/2w2vNY http://www.v3.co.uk/v3-uk/news/2259990/facebook... via @V3_co_uk Facebook attempts to pacify privacy fears following launch of Home http://ow.ly/2w2vNY	**2** clicks
3	Apr 24, 2013	http://ow.ly/2wnCUP http://www.v3.co.uk/v3-uk/news/2263577/syrian-e... via @V3_co_uk Syrian Electronic Army strikes again with cyber attack on the Associated Press http://ow.ly/2wnCUP	**1** clicks
4	Apr 20, 2013	http://ow.ly/2wigql http://feedproxy.google.com/~r/SplashMedia/~3/0... via @splashmedialp Splash Media and the Neeley School of Business at TCU Team Up to Magnify its Richards Barrentin... http://ow.ly/2wigql	**1** clicks

If you require detailed reports, HootSuite also provides paid modules that require points. One of the most important reports is the **Twitter Sentiment** report that shows the sentiment of users about a specific word or brand. In the following example, we have used **Pepsi** as the keyword and have generated a sentiment report.

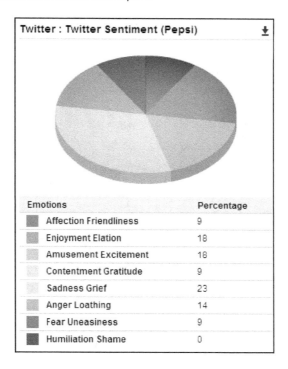

Twitter : Twitter Sentiment (Pepsi)	
Emotions	**Percentage**
Affection Friendliness	9
Enjoyment Elation	18
Amusement Excitement	18
Contentment Gratitude	9
Sadness Grief	23
Anger Loathing	14
Fear Uneasiness	9
Humiliation Shame	0

A couple of more reports that can be generated at 20 points each are **Retweet-Detailed** and **Mentions-Detailed** reports. The **Retweet-Detailed** report creates a line graph showing the growth in retweets and a list of tweets that received the highest numbers of retweets.

The **Mentions-Detailed** report also generates a line graph depicting the increase in the number of mentions over a period of time and a list of users who mentioned your Twitter handle. The user with the highest Klout score is placed at the top of this list.

The **Follower Growth-Count** report creates a line graph that shows the increase in your number of Twitter followers. In addition to the daily increase/decrease of followers, this list also shows the average daily growth in followers and the total number of followers.

For LinkedIn company pages, you can create **Snapshot** and **Company Update Engagement** reports. Each of these reports costs 10 points. A **Snapshot** report covers the number of total and new followers, and the percentage increase in their numbers. It also shows statistics over impressions and engagement. However, these statistics are already available to page administrators directly from LinkedIn.

The **Company Update Engagement** report shows the posts and the number of likes and comments received on each one of them. This is helpful for marketers to understand what is being read and liked by the page followers. Messaging can be edited as per the results from this report.

LinkedIn : Company Update Engagement			
Date ▾	Update ⇕	Likes ⇕	Comments ⇕
Feb 1, 17:02	How social media and mobile devices are changing the travel industry: http://ow.ly/hj8rv	12	21
Feb 1, 14:02	Your greatest brand advocates are right under your nose: http://owl.li/hjlxw	18	4
Jan 30, 17:02	Pleased to release HootSuite in Korean. Enjoy! http://ow.ly/hf9lh	7	0
Jan 30, 17:02	Pleased to release HootSuite in Korean. Enjoy! http://ow.ly/hf9lh	3	5
Jan 30, 16:02	3 social media tips for online marketers on the go: http://ow.ly/hf4lj	12	17
Jan 28, 17:02	You just found your second Super Bowl screen: http://ow.ly/h8VSA Super Bowl social media tracker	9	11
Jan 28, 16:06	Have you wished your CM a happy Community Manager Appreciation Day? http://ow.ly/hc18X	21	7
Jan 28, 16:06	Have you wished your CM a happy Community Manager Appreciation Day? http://ow.ly/hc18X	15	12
Jan 27, 22:01	5 free resources for building a winning community: http://ow.ly/h8wfp	6	4
Jan 27, 8:30	Instagram, YouTube, Tumblr - Have you installed these apps in HootSuite? http://owl.li/h8Sx4 Learn how in a free webinar	21	6

How it works...

Businesses have started to acknowledge the importance of social media but the problem to identify actual ROI and its effects on sales is still unclear.

The number of retweets, favorites, likes on Facebook posts, shares, or comments may not be enough to justify efforts and money invested in social media. So it is important to link social media to bigger departmental or organizational goals. It is very important to create a relation ship between conversation and conversion.

HootSuite reporting gives a detailed analysis of your social media presence, activities, target audience, demographics, and other details that help you to make crucial business decisions.

There's more...

You may check the price of all HootSuite's analytics modules in points and their descriptions from the following link `http://bit.ly/1c6l9Br`.

Implementing additional options to excel in social media (Advanced)

These additional tips will help you hone your skills of using HootSuite and add value to your work.

How to do it...

1. Use search options.
2. Monitor competitors' accounts.
3. Use a location search.

How it works...

HootSuite provides you with an option to search in Twitter and Facebook from its dashboard itself. This feature remains visible on the ribbon of the HootSuite dashboard and is placed in the top-right corner with a magnifying glass icon.

You can perform three types of searches using this option without leaving the HootSuite dashboard. By default, when you open this dropdown by clicking on its icon, it will show the latest trending topics on Twitter. These features are an extension of the Twitter search in the dashboard, and thus, give the same results as those in Twitter.

It allows you to search for any keyword or phrase with an advanced argument or operators to fine-tune your search query. Refer to the following table to see some examples of using operators on HootSuite's search and you can edit them as per your requirements.

Operator	Result
learn HootSuite	Containing both learn and HootSuite
good luck	Containing the exact phrase good luck
lion or tiger	Containing either lion or tiger or both
sun –flower	Containing sun but not flower
#marketing	Containing hashtag marketing
from:sachin_rt	Sent from person sachin_rt
to:thekunalmathur	Sent to person thekunalmathur
@avinash	Referring to person avinash
hockey since:2013-04-20	Containing hockey and sent since 2013-04-20 date
coffee until:2013-04-20	Containing coffee and sent until 2013-04-20 date
match -lost :)	Containing match but not lost and with positive attitude
shopping :(	Containing shopping and with a negative attitude
mobiles?	Containing mobiles and asking a question
party filter:links	Containing party and linking to URLs

HootSuite also allows you to search for Twitter users from within the dashboard. To perform this search, click on the magnifying glass icon and then click on the Twitter icon to select **Find Twitter Users**. You can either type the Twitter username or the user's name to perform the search.

Facebook's trends or topics can also be monitored from the HootSuite dashboard. To perform this search, click on the magnifying glass icon and then click on the Twitter icon to select the **Search Facebook** option. This will give you all the topics that have been discussed on Facebook at that point in time.

You can save the **Search Twitter** and **Search Facebook** streams for regular monitoring by clicking on the **Save as Stream** button provided at the end of the drop-down box when you search for a query.

These search results will be created as a stream in the existing opened tab that will help you to constantly get updated information with the specific keyword or phrase. You can also track conversations about your brand or competitor monitoring using this option right from your HootSuite dashboard.

Create keywords with your brand name, product name, and hashtags, and save them in a separate tab to track a conversation about you. With the help of these streams, you will be able to instantly respond to queries from your clients or provide answers to your prospects. In the following example, **Coca Cola**, **CocaColaCo**, **"diet coke"**, and **Fanta** are being tracked in different streams using search keywords. Each stream will show recent conversations about a brand.

Similarly, you can track conversations about your competitors that will enable you to understand general feedback of their clients. In continuation of the previous example, Pepsi Co. is the closest competitor of Coca Cola Co. We are tracking the **Pepsi**, **PepsiCo**, **"diet pepsi"**, and **"Mountain Dew"** keywords in a separate tab.

You can also include the negative attitude symbol:(to these searches to find unhappy or dissatisfied customers for your or a competitor's brand. Similarly, a ? operator with your searches can help you find questions that people are asking about your brand. As per your requirements, you can use any search operators explained earlier in this recipe to fine-tune your results.

If you are a business owner who needs to provide customers with directions to walk to your premises, nothing is more helpful than Geo Search. You can use this option by clicking on the magnifying glass icon, entering queries in the search box, and clicking on the cross-hairs icon (highlighted in the following screenshot):

This will provide you with results within a 25-kilometer radius of your location. Please note that this option requires your permission to read your location from the browser. This helps you bring customers from the vicinity to your stores, shops, or outlets.

Thank you for buying
Social Media Marketing with HootSuite

About Packt Publishing

Packt, pronounced 'packed', published its first book "*Mastering phpMyAdmin for Effective MySQL Management*" in April 2004 and subsequently continued to specialize in publishing highly focused books on specific technologies and solutions.

Our books and publications share the experiences of your fellow IT professionals in adapting and customizing today's systems, applications, and frameworks. Our solution based books give you the knowledge and power to customize the software and technologies you're using to get the job done. Packt books are more specific and less general than the IT books you have seen in the past. Our unique business model allows us to bring you more focused information, giving you more of what you need to know, and less of what you don't.

Packt is a modern, yet unique publishing company, which focuses on producing quality, cutting-edge books for communities of developers, administrators, and newbies alike. For more information, please visit our website: www.packtpub.com.

Writing for Packt

We welcome all inquiries from people who are interested in authoring. Book proposals should be sent to author@packtpub.com. If your book idea is still at an early stage and you would like to discuss it first before writing a formal book proposal, contact us; one of our commissioning editors will get in touch with you.

We're not just looking for published authors; if you have strong technical skills but no writing experience, our experienced editors can help you develop a writing career, or simply get some additional reward for your expertise.

Social Media for WordPress Beginner's Guide

ISBN: 978-1-84719-980-5   Paperback: 166 pages

A quicker way to build communities, engage members, and promote your site

1. Integrate automated key marketing techniques

2. Examine analytical data to measure social engagement

3. Understand the core principles of establishing meaningful social connections

Drupal 6 Social Networking

ISBN: 978-1-84719-610-1   Paperback: 312 pages

Build a social or community web site with friends lists, groups, custom user profiles, and much more

1. Step-by-step instructions for putting together a social networking site with Drupal 6

2. Customize your Drupal installation with modules and themes to match the needs of almost any social networking site

3. Allow users to collaborate and interact with each other on your site

Please check **www.PacktPub.com** for information on our titles

Elgg 1.8 Social Networking

ISBN: 978-1-84951-130-8   Paperback: 400 pages

Create, customize, and deploy your very own social networking site with Elgg

1. An updated version of the very first book on Elgg

2. Detailed and easy-to-understand analysis on building your very own social networking site with Elgg

3. Explore the vast range of Elgg's social networking capabilities including communities, sharing, profiles, and relationships

ASP.NET 4 Social Networking

ISBN: 978-1-84969-082-9   Paperback: 484 pages

A truly hands-on book for Microsoft ASP.NET 4 Developers

1. Create a full-featured, enterprise-grade social network using ASP.NET 4.0

2. Learn key new ASP.NET and .NET Framework concepts like Managed Extensibility Framework (MEF), Entity Framework 4.0, LINQ, AJAX, C# 4.0, ASP.NET Routing, n-tier architectures, and MVP in a practical, hands-on way.

3. Build friends lists, messaging systems, user profiles, blogs, forums, groups, and more

Please check **www.PacktPub.com** for information on our titles